MICHAEL
LEGEND · HERO · ICON
JACKSON
A TRIBUTE TO THE KING OF POP

MICHAEL
LEGEND · HERO · ICON
JACKSON
A TRIBUTE TO THE KING OF POP

JAMES ALDIS

HarperCollins*Publishers*

CONTENTS

Introduction

Michael Jackson was without doubt the greatest performer ever to have lived. In his own lifetime he

world culture itself will be felt down the ages. As a man and a performer Michael Jackson was totally unique. Influenced by the ghosts of an extraordinary childhood, he also faced unflagging public scrutiny. The media frenzy which surrounded his untimely death was already a constant presence in a life that seemed to hold so little privacy but to offer so many intriguing questions. Yet whatever the doubts and blame generated by his death, his legacy to the world will live on untarnished: as a man who wrote songs for the whole world to sing. »

'The incomparable Michael Jackson has made a bigger impact on music than any other artist in the history of music. He was magic. He was what we all strive to be.

... I love you, Michael.'

—Beyoncé Knowles

Everyone who loved Michael Jackson will carry with them their own favourite personal memories for the rest of their lives. For some it will be the first time they saw Michael perform with The Jackson 5, whilst for others it will be the memory of seeing him dance to 'Billie Jean' or watching the video to 'Thriller' for the first time. Some will remember the man the media portrayed in his final years, but to do so, or to reduce Michael Jackson to just one song, one era or one stage of his performing career, would be to deny his staggering longevity and range as an artist. In a career that spanned many genres, including soul, disco, rock and pop, he truly was the King, a crowned genius overlooking an immense musical terrain.

KEY FACTS:

Name: Michael Joseph Jackson

Born: 29 August 1958

Died: 25 June 2009

Parents: Joseph Walter Jackson and Katherine Esther Jackson

Siblings: Rebbie (b. 29 May 1950), Jackie (b. 4 May 1951), Tito (b. 15 October 1953), Jermaine (b. 11 December 1954), La Toya (b. 29 May 1956), Marlon (b. 12 March 1957), Randy (b. 29 October 1961) and Janet (b. 16 May 1966)

Children: Prince Michael Joseph Jackson Jr., Paris Michael Katherine Jackson, Prince Michael Jackson II (also known as 'Blanket')

Honours: Michael was inducted into the Rock and Roll Hall of Fame twice and received 13 Grammy Awards throughout his career.

'What is a genius? What is a living legend? What is a megastar? Michael Jackson – that's all … I think he is one of the finest people to hit this planet, and, in my estimation, he is the true King of Pop, Rock and Soul.'

– Elizabeth Taylor

'I've never seen anybody like Michael. He is an emotional star child.'

– Steven Spielberg

Was Michael destined for his success? His talents shone so brightly from such an early age that it was perhaps inevitable that they would someday be recognized. However, few artists before or since have been shepherded so forcefully towards the stage, with music becoming an all-consuming focus of their life. It is impossible to understand Michael Jackson the man without first understanding Michael Jackson the boy, as the boy played such a strong role in the life of the man.

In this tribute to Michael Jackson the legend, we take an overview of his career, his humble background and difficult childhood, his meteoric rise to fame with The Jackson 5 and his even more vertiginous ascent to global recognition as a solo artist. We'll see records broken and hearts broken in the story of a life that was like no other …

Following page: Michael poses with his younger sister, Janet, at the family home in the Hollywood Hills, December 1972. The two were to share a uniquely close relationship with one another throughout their lives.

CAREER CHRONOLOGY

Michael scores his first number 1 single as a solo artist with 'Ben'.

29 August 1958
Michael Joseph Jackson is born to parents Joe and Katherine Jackson in Gary, Indiana, USA.

1962
Michael's father organizes a musical group comprising his sons Tito, Jermaine and Jackie. Initially called 'The Jackson Brothers', they are soon after joined by younger brothers Marlon and Michael, becoming 'The Jackson Five'.

1970
'The Jackson 5' are launched under new label Motown and release 'I Want You Back', 'ABC', 'The Love You Save' and 'I'll Be There' – they all reach the top spot, thereby setting a world first.

6 November 1971
Michael Jackson releases his first solo single, 'Got to Be There'.

24 October 1978
Michael stars as the 'Scarecrow' in the movie adaptation of stage musical *The Wiz* with Diana Ross and meets Quincy Jones.

10 August 1979
Michael releases his first solo album as an adult, *Off the Wall*, marking his first collaboration with Quincy Jones. The album goes platinum while singles 'Don't Stop 'til You Get Enough' and 'Rock with You' top the charts.

30 November 1982
Michael releases the album *Thriller*, which goes on to become the biggest-selling album of all time. It remains in the charts for two years and hits top spots worldwide.

'Beat It', 'Billie Jean', 'The Girl Is Mine', 'Wanna Be Startin' Somethin'', 'Human Nature' and 'P.Y.T. (Pretty Young Thing)' all reach number 1 in the charts.

The music video to 'Billie Jean' becomes the first video by a black artist to be aired regularly on channel MTV, while the video for *Thriller* is now widely accepted as the greatest music video of all time.

23 February 1983
Jackson wins 8 Grammy Awards and agrees a lucrative advertising deal with Pepsi Cola.

6 July 1984

Michael releases his final studio album with the Jacksons, *Victory*.

31 August 1987

Michael's new album, *Bad*, is released, debuting at number 1 in the charts. The world tour which supports it becomes the highest-grossing tour of all time.

Singles released from the album, 'I Just Can't Stop Loving You', 'Bad', 'The Way You Make Me Feel', 'Man in the Mirror' and 'Dirty Diana', all reach number 1.

1988

Jackson moves into his new California home, the Neverland Ranch, and publishes his autobiography, *Moonwalk*.

26 November 1991

Michael's *Dangerous* album is released, with single 'Black or White' debuting at number 1.

31 January 1993

Michael's half-time performance at Super Bowl XXVII gains the highest viewing figures in the history of US television.

26 May 1994

Michael marries Lisa Marie Presley, daughter of Elvis Presley. The marriage ends amicably two years later.

20 June 1995

Jackson releases *HIStory: Past, Present and Future, Book I*, a two-CD album including 15 of his greatest hits and 15 new songs.

14 November 1996

Michael marries Debbie Rowe. Together they have two children, Prince Michael Jackson, Jr. and Paris Michael Katherine Jackson. The couple divorce in October 2000.

19 March 2001

Michael is inducted into the Rock and Roll Hall of Fame. Later that year he holds a concert at Madison Square Garden to celebrate his 30 years as a solo artist. Also

that year, Michael releases his album *Invincible*.

21 February 2002

Prince Michael II ('Blanket') born.

5 March 2009

Michael announces a return to the public arena with a series of concerts at London's O2 Arena.

25 June 2009

Michael Jackson dies following a heart attack at his home in California.

1 From the steelworks to Hitsville

Michael Jackson's career as a performer began incredibly early. Although fellow musicians Stevie Wonder and Donny Osmond had been child stars, Michael was different: he immediately exploded onto the popular music scene and caught the public's attention in a way that had never been seen before, thanks to his unmatched vocal gifts and performing skills. The intense focus on his career that characterized his childhood and adolescence later took a toll on him, it being at once both the making and – in the view of many – the breaking of him. Deprived of a normal childhood and subject to the exhausting demands of constant practice and the ambitions of his family, Michael was catapulted into the limelight at an age when most kids would be playing in the street or at school.

MICHAEL'S EARLY LIFE AND THE HISTORY OF THE JACKSON FIVE

'When you're a show business child, you really don't have the maturity to understand a great deal of what is going on around you. People make a lot of decisions concerning your life when you're out of the room. So here's what I remember. I remember singing at the top of my voice and dancing with real joy and working too hard for a child.'

— Michael Jackson

'If you enter this world knowing you are loved and you leave this world knowing the same, then everything that happens in between can be dealt with.'

– Michael Jackson

A HUMBLE BACKGROUND

The four boys who made up the band were amongst the eldest of a family of nine, born to Joe and Katherine Jackson. Joe's background as a steel-worker in Gary, Indiana, offered the children a humble start in life, with the entire family squeezed into a house of just three rooms, but his passion for developing the unique set of gifts his children possessed was to be the catalyst that raised the family above and beyond their surroundings in a way that no-one could ever have foreseen.

Joe played guitar in a band called The Falcons with his brother. Their rock 'n' roll covers of Otis Redding, Little Richard and Chuck Berry could be heard in the house at weekends when the band came over to rehearse and must have had an impressive influence on the young Jackson flock; meanwhile, mother Katherine played clarinet and piano, evidence of a shared musical gift that ran through the family.

Left: The Jackson children, with the exception of Jermaine, pose together. Left to right: (back row) Rebbie, Jackie, Marlon, Tito, (front row) Michael, Janet, Randy and La Toya.

Above left: The small family home on Jackson street.
Above right: Michael aged three.

'I remember going to the record studio and there was a park across the street and I'd see all the children playing and I would cry because it would make me sad that I would have to work instead.'
– Michael Jackson

The kids were fascinated by their dad's skill with the guitar, and whenever he left the house they would sneak to the closet where he kept it safely hidden and pull it out to practise on. Tito, Jackie and Jermaine would all try out scales and chords, trying to emulate the sounds their father made and the tunes they had heard on the radio. Then one day Joe returned to find a string broken on the guitar. Initially angry, he said to Tito, 'Let me see what you can do.' When Tito then showed how adept he'd become, Joe realized that the kids hadn't just been fooling around and were taking music seriously. The three oldest brothers were determined to show their dad their ability and, over time, with the encouragement of their mum, Joe let them start spending time together rehearsing.

As much as the band was a tight unit of five, they were always part of a larger clan.
Above, younger brother Randy joins his older siblings while below they are joined by Janet.
Above right: Michael the child and Michael the young man. Perhaps a way to keep his
childhood self alive, Michael frequently sported a Mickey Mouse design on his clothes.

A BAND OF BROTHERS

Michael was still just three or four years old when the band was formed, but there was no question over his eventual inclusion within the line-up – his talents shone as brightly as any star in the sky. His precocious vocal talent and ability to play the bongos meant that he was a surefire member of the team. The band's first incarnation in 1964 consisted of brothers Jackie, Tito and Jermaine, under the name The Jackson Brothers, but the following year Michael, aged five, and brother Marlon joined the group, establishing a set-up that would remain in place for the following decade. Initially, the band covered popular soul and R&B songs of the day, absorbing influences from James Brown to Sly and the Family Stone.

'I've always joked that I didn't ask to sing and dance, but it's true. When I open my mouth, music comes out.'

– Michael Jackson

Seeing their potential, Joe began to spend less time with The Falcons and more time developing his children's fledgling act. He began putting them forward for performances at talent contests and amateur nights, and before long they were developing both a reputation and a well-practised edge. Soon their live performances would be captured for posterity as Joe clinched a deal with a local recording studio and label named Steeltown. Their first release, a single entitled 'Big Boy', featured nine-year-old Michael on vocals, and helped them gain a foothold with larger concert venues, such as the Apollo Theater in New York and some of Chicago's biggest talent shows.

Right: Michael as a freshman in 1973 at Montclair College Preparatory School in Van Nuys, California.

Above left: The kids pose in front of a huge J5 sculpture graffitied with their names.

Above right: The band at one of many awards ceremonies. Here they are at the NAACP Image Awards, established for the advancement of coloured people within the arts.

A STAGE EDUCATION

They began touring venues on the 'chitlin' circuit' of black nightclubs throughout the east and south of the country, and were regularly billed alongside major acts of the day, such as James Brown. For young Michael, watching from the wings, this became his school. Deprived of a normal classroom education Michael would instead carefully watch James Brown's performances: he would absorb every single step, every single movement, every twist, turn, grind and emotion, packing it into his memory, mesmerized by its brilliance.

Having worked the 'chitlin' circuit', The Jacksons were already familiar with life on the road by the time a phone call came out of the blue that would mean a long journey to Detroit. They had been invited to go to Motown.

'The greatest education in the world is watching the masters at work.'
– Michael Jackson

MOTOWN

Perhaps it was fate that Michael became the performer he ultimately grew into, but his father's drive to secure a recording contract to marry success to his children's talents almost inevitably led them to one of the most famous homes of popular music in the late 1960s and early 1970s – Motown.

LIST OF MOTOWN NUMBER 1s…

1960s

YEAR	SONG	PERFORMER	WEEKS AT NO. 1
1961	'Please Mr. Postman'	The Marvelettes	1
1963	'Fingertips – Pt. 2'	Little Stevie Wonder	3
1964	'My Guy'	Mary Wells	2
1964	'Where Did Our Love Go'	The Supremes	2
1964	'Baby Love'	The Supremes	4
1964	'Come See About Me'	The Supremes	2
1965	'My Girl'	The Temptations	1
1965	'Stop! In the Name of Love'	The Supremes	2
1965	'Back in My Arms Again'	The Supremes	1
1965	'I Can't Help Myself'	Four Tops	2
1965	'I Hear a Symphony'	The Supremes	2
1966	'You Can't Hurry Love'	The Supremes	2
1966	'Reach Out I'll Be There'	Four Tops	2
1966	'You Keep Me Hangin' On'	The Supremes	2
1967	'Love is Here and Now You're Gone'	The Supremes	1
1967	'The Happening'	The Supremes	1
1968	'Love Child'	Diana Ross & The Supremes	2
1968	'I Heard it Through the Grapevine'	Marvin Gaye	7
1969	'I Can't Get Next to You'	The Temptations	2
1969	'Someday We'll Be Together'	Diana Ross & The Supremes	1

1970s

YEAR	SONG	PERFORMER	WEEKS IN CHART
1970	'I Want You Back'	The Jackson 5	1
1970	'ABC'	The Jackson 5	2
1970	'The Love You Save'	The Jackson 5	2
1970	'War'	Edwin Starr	3
1970	'Ain't No Mountain High Enough'	Diana Ross	3
1970	'I'll Be There'	The Jackson 5	5
1970	'The Tears of a Clown'	Smokey Robinson & The Miracles	2
1971	'Just My Imagination'	The Temptations	2
1972	'Ben'	Michael Jackson	1
1972	'Papa Was a Rollin' Stone'	The Temptations	1
1973	'Superstition'	Stevie Wonder	1
1973	'You Are the Sunshine of My Life'	Stevie Wonder	1
1973	'Touch Me in the Morning'	Diana Ross	1
1973	'Let's Get It On'	Marvin Gaye	2
1973	'Keep On Truckin' (Pt. 1)'	Eddie Kendricks	2
1974	'You Haven't Done Nothin''	Stevie Wonder	1
1976	'Theme from Mahogany (Do You Know Where You're Going To)'	Diana Ross	1
1976	'Love Machine (Pt. 1)'	The Miracles	1
1976	'Love Hangover'	Diana Ross	2
1977	'I Wish'	Stevie Wonder	1
1977	'Don't Leave Me This Way'	Thelma Houston	1
1977	'Sir Duke'	Stevie Wonder	3
1977	'Got to Give it Up (Pt. 1)'	Marvin Gaye	1
1978	'Three Times a Lady'	The Commodores	2
1979	'Still'	The Commodores	1

1980s

YEAR	SONG	PERFORMER	WEEKS IN CHART
1980	'Upside Down'	Diana Ross	4
1981	'Endless Love'	Diana Ross & Lionel Ritchie	9
1982	'Truly'	Lionel Ritchie	2
1983	'All Night Long (All Night)'	Lionel Ritchie	4
1984	'Hello'	Lionel Ritchie	2
1984	'I Just Called to Say I Love You'	Stevie Wonder	3
1985	'Part-Time Lover'	Stevie Wonder	1
1985	'Say You, Say Me'	Lionel Ritchie	4

1990s

YEAR	SONG	PERFORMER	WEEKS IN CHART
1992	'End of the Road'	Boyz II Men	13
1994	'I'll Make Love to You'	Boyz II Men	14
1994	'On Bended Knee'	Boyz II Men	6
1997	'4 Seasons of Loneliness'	Boyz II Men	1

The very word 'Motown' has become synonymous with great music thanks to the almost constant stream of hit songs the label produced. But it was also the first label to end the segregation within the music industry – for the first time music by black musicians and groups was being sold outside their traditional markets and across the world. It effectively ended a period of musical apartheid on the strength of the songs themselves and the genius of their performers, and no act typified this more than The Jackson 5, who would go on to become one of the label's most popular acts and the first group of teen idols to appeal widely to both black and white kids.

'I recognized the bridges that we crossed, the racial problems and the barriers that we broke down with music.'

– Smokey Robinson

Motown's emergence took place at the same time as America was going through a wider set of social changes, thanks to the Civil Rights Movement that had been born in the sixties and was led by heroes such as Martin Luther King Jr. Culturally, the sands were shifting and integration of white and black people was gradually becoming possible throughout the different levels of life; the success of Motown, with its jubilant, infectious rhythms, encapsulated the feeling that a change was coming and could not be held back. The universality of its appeal became a musical expression of the fact that everyone had a right to share the same chances, opportunities and freedoms in life – an eternal truth which runs through many of the lyrics that Michael composed.

Above: **Legendary producer Berry Gordy with another legend, Diana Ross.**

The label was founded in Detroit in 1959 by Berry Gordy Jr., at first under the name Tamla Records and then as the Motown Record Corporation, with just an $800 loan from his family. From this tiny acorn grew a mighty oak that stands tall to this day. The small house Berry and his team occupied on West Grand Boulevard rapidly became known as 'Hitsville, USA'.

Throughout the sixties they established the 'Motown Sound' with a stream of successes. Their first number 1 hit in the US *Billboard* R&B charts came with 'Shop Around' by The Miracles, which went on to sell over a million copies. Just a year later they scored their first number 1 pop smash with 'Please Mr. Postman'. In the decade that followed, between 1961 and 1971, Motown had an astonishing 110 top ten hits, with artists like Marvin Gaye, Stevie Wonder, Diana Ross & the Supremes and The Four Tops flocking to join the ranks.

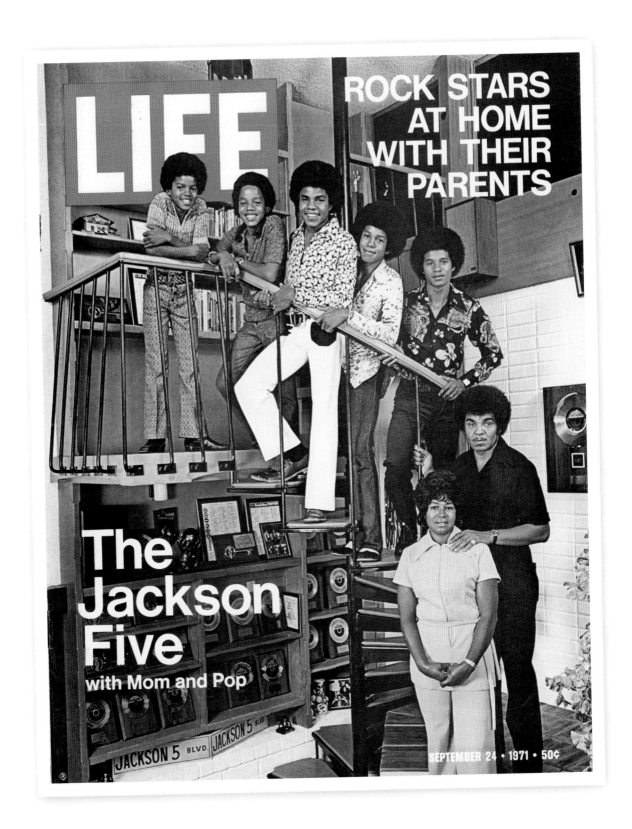

The Jackson Five with Mom and Pop

The Jacksons already had a recording contract in place, but the invitation to audition for Motown was something no-one in their right mind would turn down.

Gladys Knight, already a star of the Motown label, had recommended to Berry Gordy that he sign the band after seeing them perform, but he initially showed reluctance due to their age (as well as the presence of another young star under his wings, the immensely talented Stevie Wonder). However, after seeing the videotaped audition, Berry set about bringing them under his tutelage. The Jackson Five signed with Gordy in 1969, changing their name to The Jackson 5 at the same time.

They were moved out to California, where they began an intensive period of song-writing, rehearsing and media-training, preparing them for their forthcoming launch into the pop arena. Berry and the staff of Motown meanwhile set about generating a marketing and publicity storm to accompany their entrance into this new world.

What effect the turbulence of these years had on the young Michael and his brothers is unknown, but as exciting as it must have been, the move to California must also

have been disorientating. At first, whilst looking for a place to live, the five brothers briefly lodged with Diana Ross. It wasn't until the following year that father Joseph was finally able to move to California with his wife and four other children to join the group.

Despite the turbulence, at last the family had been offered a chance to test their mettle and be given the ultimate push towards stardom.

Above: **The camera was always on Michael, even when at home.**

THE JACKSON 5

Berry Gordy was to describe The Jackson 5 as 'the last big stars to come rolling off my assembly line'. Whether he was aware at the time that they would become the megastars they did is unknown, but the band exploded into the new decade with hit after hit – their first four singles with Motown were all released in the same year of 1970 and went in at number 1, thereby setting a record and making music history.

The band had been playing together for much of the sixties, but it was only when they teamed up with Gordy that their potential as a popular super-group was realized. Their incredible choreography and harmonized singing set stages alight, but it was 11-year-old Michael who caught the greatest portion of the public's affection. So young and yet so talented, Michael instantly became a phenomenon, loved by children and adults alike.

'I Want You Back', 'ABC', 'The Love You Save' and 'I'll Be There' all became number I singles in the US charts.

'ABC' knocked The Beatles' 'Let It Be' off the top spot when it was released in April 1970

'ABC' and 'I Want You Back' are among the Rock and Roll Hall of Fame's 500 Songs that Shaped Rock and Roll.

'I met Michael Jackson at the age of eight – when his father and my new friend, Joe Jackson, first began to bring the Jackson 5 to Chicago from their home in Gary, Indiana, for concert appearances ... Michael's personal crescendo of amazing power as an entertainer was clear and unmistakable.'

– Don Cornelius, creator of the television show, *Soul Train*

'My brothers and I –
our whole family – were very
proud. We had created a new
sound for a new decade. It was
the first time in recording
history that a bunch of kids
had made so many
hit records.'

– Michael Jackson

Following the release of 'I Want You Back' in January 1970 a rollercoaster was set in motion. In the space of a few months Jacksonmania was sweeping the country, and by the end of the year the band were a headline act, consistently performing to vast audiences at sell-out concerts. Their kid-friendly, cheerful image made them a huge pull, and they rapidly became regular guests on popular TV shows such as *The Ed Sullivan Show*. Before long a Saturday morning cartoon show based on their lives would appear, cementing their popularity among children.

The frenetic days and months of touring that followed the record releases brought the band of brothers closer together. Playing huge venues such as Madison Square Garden and the Los Angeles Forum was a thrill, but the non-stop gigs (in 1971 they played over 40 different cities during the summer period alone) led to a lot of time on the road. To alleviate boredom and to cheer themselves up the brothers would clown around. Going through such an extraordinary experience was like a baptism of sorts – they were all in it together, so had to support one another to get through.

Controversy surrounded The Jacksons' tour for the album Victory. Amidst huge public demand, ticket prices were set at the (then) very high price of $30. In response, Michael announced that he would be donating his entire share of the proceeds – estimated at $5m – to charity.

Left: Michael singing on the *Victory* tour in 1984. He performed many of his solo songs as part of the tour.
Below: With disco queen Donna Summer.

THE DECADE OF DISCO

The band evolved with their times, going on to develop fresh hits that tapped into the disco movement, and although major changes to the band would take place throughout the seventies – Jermaine Jackson parted company with the group to launch a solo career and was replaced by his brother Randy; the band switched labels, first to join the Philadelphia International Records label and then Epic Records, in the process changing their name to simply The Jacksons – what remained constant was their popularity and their consistent creative brilliance. Albums like *Destiny* (1978), *Triumph* (1980) and *Victory* (1984) sealed their place in music history, with *Destiny*'s 'Blame It on the Boogie' becoming a staple of dancehalls for the next 30 years, and the album itself, completely self-produced and written by the group, proving to the industry that The Jacksons were unmatched in their creative abilities.

Yet *Victory* was to be the last project with which Michael would be involved. Long before this point his solo career had already shown signs of going stratospheric.

2 The 1980s

was the decade in which Michael went from child star to adult mega-star. Whilst retaining strong ties to his family and The Jacksons, Michael branched out as a performer, establishing a legendary partnership with producer Quincy Jones and writing some of the 20th century's greatest ever pop songs. Michael began the decade as a prince but ended it as the undisputed King of Pop.

As Michael grew into his teens his stage charisma and unmatched singing and dancing abilities also grew. In a stunning precursor of his later performance of the 'Moonwalk', Michael's robotic dance in 1974's 'Dancing Machine' established a move that has been imitated around the world ever since.

His presence on stage and his ability to excite an audience were already singling him out as a star that outshone every other. It would be just a matter of a few short years before his mighty talent would be unleashed on the world.

'… when we sang 'Dancing Machine' on *Soul Train* I did a streetstyle dance move called the Robot … Overnight, 'Dancing Machine' rose to the top of the charts, and within a few days it seemed that every kid in the United States was doing the Robot.'

– Michael Jackson

Left to right: From having been thrust into the limelight at such an early age, Michael's confidence as a performer and as an individual seemed to grow exponentially throughout his adolescence, as he grew into the adult performer that dominated the 1980s.
Below left: Michael arriving at the Golden Globes awards ceremony with his Dad.
Below centre and right: The Jackson 5 with younger brother Randy (wearing a straw hat).

A SHINING LIGHT

Young Michael was not only leader of the band but was also the undoubted favourite of the act. From an early stage it was clear that he had the potential to go beyond the success of The Jackson 5, and as early as 1971 that potential was chased.

The single 'Got to Be There' was released towards the end of 1971, with the album it took its name from following in January the next year. This was Michael's first solo venture and at the age of just thirteen it must have been an incredible experience for him to be thrust, standing alone, into the limelight. The album's title track and the classic 'Rockin' Robin' both

became hits whilst the album peaked at number 14 in the US pop charts. However, it was with his second album that Michael scored his first taste of solo superstardom.

The album *Ben* was released in August 1972 and its title track became an instant smash, hitting the number 1 spot in both the US and Australia (where it spent eight weeks at the top), and selling over a million copies. As the theme song to a major film of the same name, the song also afforded Michael his first major award, winning a Golden Globe for Best Song and a nomination for Best Original Song at the Academy Awards.

FROM THE PRINCE OF POP TO THE KING OF POP

'It's staggering what a person can do if they only try.'

— Michael Jackson

FOLLOWING THE YELLOW-BRICK ROAD

In 1978 Michael starred alongside Diana Ross and Richard Pryor in a hugely successful movie, *The Wiz*. A musical version of the classic *The Wizard of Oz*, *The Wiz* changed the setting of the tale from Kansas to New York City and adopted an entirely African-American cast. Michael's performance as the Scarecrow was critically well received but it was his introduction to music producer Quincy Jones that was to prove the most fateful aspect of his involvement with the film.

Quincy became friends with Michael during the making of the film, and as a result of their collaboration Michael asked Quincy to work with him on producing his fifth solo album.

Above and above right: **Michael attending the premiere of *The Wiz*.**
Right: **In costume as the Scarecrow.**
Following pages: **On stage at the opening night of the 1984 *Victory* tour.**

OFF THE WALL

The result of their collaboration was the album *Off the Wall*. It sold a staggering 20 million copies around the world, with two of its songs released as singles hitting the number 1 spot and a further two making it into the top ten. Although Michael had the privilege of working with some other great artists during the writing of the album, including Paul McCartney and Stevie Wonder, he also wrote material for the album himself, including the first single to be released, 'Don't Stop 'til You Get Enough', which earned Michael his first number 1 hit since 'Ben'. The song also garnered critical acclaim, winning Michael an American Music Award as well as a Grammy Award.

'I think every child star suffers through this period because you're not the cute and charming child that you were. You start to grow, and they want to keep you little forever.'

– Michael Jackson

'A slick, sophisticated R&B-pop showcase with a definite disco slant.'
— Stephen Holden,
Rolling Stone

A breakthrough release in many ways, 'Don't Stop 'til You Get Enough' shows Michael spreading his wings musically as his unique falsetto treatment of the melody soars above the driving disco beats below. And with an innovative video that showed Michael dancing in triplicate, the song catapulted him above and beyond the Motown roots of his teens and into a new musical space.

The album was re-released in 2001, and it has since been certified as a 7 x multi-Platinum-selling album.

Presented to
Michael Jackson
On the third day of September 1980
in commemoration of an unprecedented
4 top ten singles from the album
"OFF THE WALL"

OFF THE WALL

Release date:	10 August 1979
Producer:	Michael Jackson/Quincy Jones
Singles:	'Don't Stop 'til You Get Enough'; 'Rock with You'; 'Off the Wall'; 'She's Out of My Life'; 'Girlfriend'

PLAYLIST:

'Don't Stop 'til You Get Enough'

'Rock With You'

'Workin' Day and Night'

'Get on the Floor'

'Off the Wall'

'Girlfriend'

'She's Out of My Life'

'I Can't Help It'

'It's the Falling in Love'

'Burn This Disco Out'

'I've been told over and over that black people on the cover of magazines doesn't sell copies … Just wait. Someday those magazines are going to be begging me for an interview.'

– Michael Jackson, 1980, speaking after the release of *Off the Wall*.

Above left: Michael was a constant innovator when it came to his personal style. The tux he wore for *Off the Wall* marked a new, sophisticated adult persona.

Above right: With singer Bonnie Pointer, and sister La Toya at The American Music Awards.

BREAKING BOUNDARIES

Although *Off the Wall* had been a huge success, Michael felt that he hadn't achieved the level of success that he knew he had within him. Being over-looked for the award of Record of the Year was, Michael felt, unfair, and he also recognized that the colour of his skin was seen by many within the industry as a barrier to success. Michael was determined that his hard work could overcome any obstacles set in his path.

As a backdrop to his disappointment with *Off the Wall*, in Michael's personal life he had to contend with the challenge of moving away from his father's managerial control. On turning 21 in

1979 Michael ended his professional relationship with his father, replacing him with a new manager, the entertainment lawyer John Branca.

As Michael explained in his autobiography, 'I was beginning to feel that I was working for *him* rather than working for *me*. And on the creative side we are of two completely different minds ... All I wanted was control over my own life. And I took it.' The moment marked a significant point in Michael's career, and with his newfound creative freedom came huge energy. Perhaps it was for this reason that Michael's next project was to become a landmark in musical history: the album *Thriller*.

THRILLING AUDIENCES

Although Michael released the album *Triumph* with
The Jacksons in 1980, with its classic track 'Can You Feel It',
nothing could prepare fans for what would happen next.
The world was poised to receive the second gift of the
partnership between Michael Jackson and Quincy Jones
and a work that forever demonstrates Michael's unparalleled
musical genius: the album *Thriller*.

'Ever since I was a little boy,
I had dreamed of
creating the biggest-selling
record of all time.'

– Michael Jackson

THRILLER

Release date:	30 August 1982
Producer:	Michael Jackson/Quincy Jones
Singles:	'The Girl Is Mine'; 'Billie Jean'; 'Beat It'; 'Wanna Be Startin' Somethin''; 'Human Nature'; 'P.Y.T. (Pretty Young Thing)'; 'Thriller'

PLAYLIST:

'Wanna Be Startin' Somethin''

'Baby Be Mine'

'The Girl Is Mine'

'Thriller'

'Beat It'

'Billie Jean'

'Human Nature'

'P.Y.T. (Pretty Young Thing)'

'The Lady in My Life'

'People used to do an album where you'd get one good song, and the rest were like B-sides. They'd call them "album songs" – and I would say to myself "Why can't every song be so great that people would want to buy it as a single?"'

– Michael Jackson

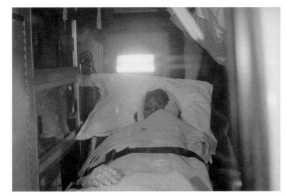

Above left: At the legendary 1984 Grammy Awards with friend and collaborator, the producer Quincy Jones.

Above right: While filming a commercial for Pepsi Cola Michael suffered second degree burns to his scalp. Michael subsequently gave a generous donation to the Brotman Medical Center in California where he had been treated.

It's impossible to overstate the success of Michael's sixth solo album. It is quite simply the bestselling album of all time. Selling over a million copies each week at its zenith, its estimated sales are now pitched between 47 and 109 million copies. Like *Off the Wall*, the album showcases Michael's versatility as an artist, with songs that cover a range of styles and genres, from disco and funk to soft rock and pop. But unlike the joy and abandon of 'Don't Stop 'til You Get Enough', *Thriller* carried an edginess that was completely new. In addition to its immense popular appeal, the album was critically acclaimed, winning Michael a record-breaking eight Grammy Awards across the genres of rock, R&B and pop, once again signalling his enormous breadth of appeal.

The dark side of *Thriller* – with its themes of loneliness and isolation – showed a new, adult facet of Michael's personality. Having been the key figure in The Jacksons' 'bubblegum soul' sound at Motown, Michael was now finally free to show his artistic individuality.

Left to right: At the 1984 Grammy Awards; with fellow Motown graduate Lionel Ritchie; Michael onstage with guitarist Eddie Van Halen, performing 'Beat It'.

THE GREATEST MUSIC VIDEO EVER MADE

Videos for the break-out songs of the album rapidly became hugely popular in their own right: the video to 'Billie Jean' was the first video by a black singer to be aired in heavy rotation on MTV, while the 14-minute video that accompanied the release of the single 'Thriller' is widely considered the greatest music video ever made. Directed by John Landis, this mini-screenplay, in which Michael alternately appears as a werecat and a zombie (in its most famous moment, dancing with a troupe of zombies) was at its time the most expensive music video ever produced, with a budget of over half a million dollars. However, proving that with high stakes come high rewards, it has since gone on to sell over nine million copies and to be acclaimed by the *Guinness World Records* as the most popular music video of all time.

AWARDS FOR THE MUSIC VIDEO OF 'THRILLER'

Year	Award	Genre	Result
1984	MTV Award	Best Overall Performance in a Video	Winner
1984	MTV Award	Best Choreography	Winner
1984	MTV Award	Viewer's Choice	Winner
1984	Grammy	Best Video Album	Winner
1985	Grammy	Best Video, Long Form	Winner
1999	MTV Award	100 Greatest Music Videos Ever Made	Number 1

'I'll never forget that night, because when I opened my eyes at the end, people were on their feet applauding. I was overwhelmed by the reaction. It felt so good.'

– Michael Jackson

MOTOWN 25 AND THE BIRTH OF A LEGEND

If one single moment can be picked out in Michael Jackson's remarkable career that saw him transform from superstar performer into living legend, it was perhaps his performance of 'Billie Jean' on Motown's televised 25th-anniversary celebrations in 1983.

The showcase event brought together a star-studded array of talent from Motown's back catalogue – The Supremes, Stevie Wonder, The Temptations and Marvin Gaye. The night offered Michael the chance to be reunited with his brothers onstage for the first time in nearly seven years. They sang a selection of their greatest hits, and the crowd went wild for them. But it was Michael's solo performance of his new single, 'Billie Jean', that sent shockwaves through the TV screens of the millions watching at home.

The performance that viewers witnessed on stage seemed to transcend anything they had ever seen before. Michael's breath-taking dancing, coupled with his vocals, was nothing short of mesmerizing. And then suddenly Michael moved in a way that seemed to defy belief: Michael 'moon-walked' across the stage, appearing to walk forward yet move backwards at the same time. For those who weren't lucky enough to number among the 47 million who witnessed the event at the time, it is impossible to conceive what impact this had. Fortunately, the brilliance of the movement and the stunning effect it had meant that it would soon become one of Michael's signature moves.

Previous pages: **A moment captured for eternity – Michael's performance at *Motown 25*.**
Opposite page: **Michael greets the crowd after a visit to Madame Tussauds in 1985.**

HOW TO DO THE MOONWALK

Illustrations by Nick McFarlane

5

ONE GIANT LEAP FOR MANKIND

With your weight on your left leg (heel still in the air), slide your right foot back until it's behind your left – now keep the sequence going, and make sure to use your head and arms to emphasise the 'walking' movement.

4

MOONWALKING

Now snap the heel of your left foot up as you simultaneously snap the heel of your right foot down (you should now be in the 'L' position again but with switched feet).

3

WE'RE ALMOST THERE

Keep your right
heel off the floor
and slide your
left foot backwards
until it's just
behind your
right foot, always
keeping your
toes in contact
with the floor.

2

ONE SMALL STEP FOR MAN ...

Slide the toes
of your right foot
back (until they
are resting
approximately a
foot behind your
left foot, forming
an 'L' position).

1

LUNAR SURFACE

Smoothness is
critical to doing
the moonwalk –
if it's your first
time try using
just your socks
on a polished
floor. Stand tall
with your feet
together.

Michael's love for animals was a constant, which eventually led to him building a zoo at Neverland. Here, he is seen with Bubbles the chimp, Louie the llama and Muscles the boa constrictor.

A MAN LIKE NO OTHER

With the release of *Thriller* and his performance at *Motown 25*, Michael appeared to have achieved many of his aspirations. Winning eight Grammy Awards at the 1984 ceremony seemed to offer the critical recognition that he had felt eluded him with *Off the Wall*. But it was as an outstanding human being as well as a performer that Michael Jackson was also becoming known. His invitation to the White House in 1984 saw him meet President Ronald Reagan and receive from him an award for his support of alcohol and drug abuse charities. The following year Michael teamed up with fellow Motown graduate Lionel Ritchie to pen the charity single 'We Are the World', the proceeds of which were donated to help famine relief in Africa (the single sold nearly 20 million copies and raised huge amounts of cash to help the needy and starving).

Left to Right: Performing 'We Are The World' at a USA for Africa benefit in 1984. Ray Charles, Billy Joel, Stevie Wonder and Paul Simon are among the famous faces; at the White House with President Ronald Reagan and his wife, Nancy; Michael with one of his most loyal, long-standing friends, the great Elizabeth Taylor.

The second half of the 1980s saw Michael Jackson cement his title as the King of Pop. With the release of his seventh album, *Bad*, in 1987, he achieved a level of stardom matched only by the likes of Elvis and The Beatles. Unfettered and free to develop himself artistically, he became a truly individual performer, amassing staggering earnings from his album sales and concerts as well as from a candid autobiography in which he spoke openly of the challenges of his childhood. In many ways the 1980s belonged to Michael Jackson.

THE KING OF POP

Michael's seventh studio album and his third collaboration with Quincy Jones came five years after the break-out success of *Thriller*. His new album, *Bad*, wasn't to achieve the same giddy heights as its predecessor but has nonetheless sold over 30 million copies since its release in 1987. In addition, an incredible five of its seven single tracks hit the number 1 spot in the US Billboard charts, more than any other album in history. The album itself was Michael's first to debut at the number 1 slot, where it subsequently spent six weeks. In the UK, the album sold over half a million copies in just five days.

More so than on any previous project, Michael had huge creative input into the album: nine of its eleven songs were written by him. Its range of sounds and moods is remarkable, with ballads such as 'Man in the Mirror' sitting alongside out-and-out pop smashes like 'Bad' and 'Smooth Criminal'.

BAD

Release date:	31 August 1987
Producer:	Michael Jackson/Quincy Jones
Singles:	'I Just Can't Stop Loving You'; 'Bad'; 'The Way You Make Me Feel'; 'Man in the Mirror'; 'Dirty Diana'; 'Another Part of Me'; 'Smooth Criminal'; 'Leave Me Alone'; 'Liberian Girl'

PLAYLIST:

'Bad'

'The Way You Make Me Feel'

'Speed Demon'

'Liberian Girl'

'Just Good Friends'

'Another Part of Me'

'Man in the Mirror'

'I Just Can't Stop Loving You'

'Dirty Diana'

'Smooth Criminal'

'I wanted to do an album that was like Tchaikovsky's *Nutcracker Suite*, so that a thousand years from now people would still be listening to it.'
– Michael Jackson

'"Man in the Mirror" is a great message. I love that song. If John Lennon was alive, he could really relate to that song because it says that if you want to make the world a better place, you have to work on yourself and change first.'

– Michael Jackson

The Princess of Hearts and the King of Pop. The two were united in their commitment to charity.

RECORD BREAKER

Like *Thriller*, *Bad* set new standards for original music videos, so it's no wonder that the videos to 'Bad' and 'Smooth Criminal' have become almost as famous in their own right as the brilliant songs they accompanied. Meanwhile, the accompanying stadium tour for the album set new records. Among 123 concerts performed in front of a total of 4.4 million people, Michael gave seven sell-out performances at Wembley Stadium in the UK in front of 504,000 people, earning himself a place in the *Guinness World Records*. He also set a new record with the reported $125 million he earned as a result of the tour, but ever the philanthropist, Michael insisted that underprivileged children were invited to the shows to watch for free, while he gave significant donations to charities on the back of the tour's earnings.

WALKING ON THE MOON

Producing *Bad* had afforded Michael the opportunity to produce another mini-film, *Moonwalker*, which featured him performing some of the album's hit songs, but it also supplied wind to the sails of success that met the publication of his autobiography, *Moonwalk*, in 1988. For the first time, Michael publicly discussed personal issues that the media had already been broaching – most prominently his plastic surgery. Rather than denying rumours, Michael revealed the extent of the surgery he had undergone, namely the work that had been done to his nose and chin. In an act of startling honesty and openness, he also spoke of the abuse that he'd suffered as a child.

Perhaps as a way to compensate for the lost childhood he hadn't been able to enjoy, in the

An aerial view of Neverland.

year after *Bad* was released Michael opened the doors of his new home near Santa Ynez, California. Here he had set about creating a unique, dreamlike space that he called the Neverland Ranch, complete with its own movie theatre, zoo and theme park. Jackson named his new home after the fantasy island of Neverland from J.M. Barrie's *Peter Pan*. The ranch was to remain Jackson's home for the next twenty years.

'When we worked together on *Bad*, I was in awe of his absolute mastery of movement on the one hand, and of the music on the other. Every step he took was absolutely precise and fluid at the same time. It was like watching quicksilver in motion.'

– Film director Martin Scorsese

Michael's autobiography, *Moonwalk*, reached the top of the *New York Times* bestseller list. It took four years to write, and due to the massive public interest it was published in secret – at the printing plant where the book was printed it was given the codename 'Neil Armstrong', after the astronaut who famously first walked on the moon.

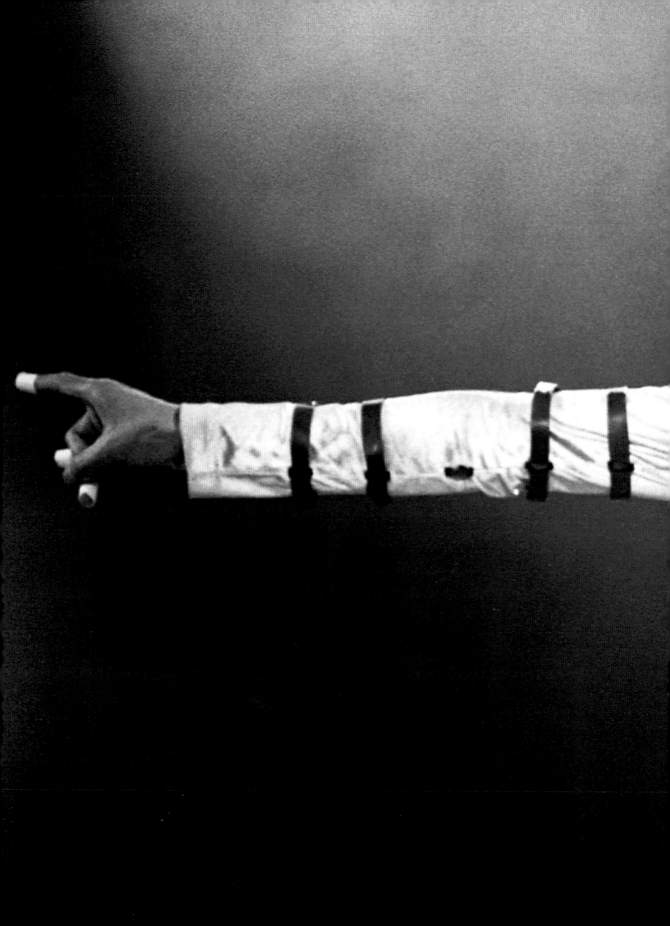

DANGEROUS

As the world entered a new decade, Michael Jackson began work on his eighth studio album; one which would take him a record 16 months to complete. *Dangerous* was released in November 1991 and became Michael's second album to debut at the top slot on the *Billboard* album chart, going on to spend four consecutive weeks there. Since its release the record has sold more than its immediate predecessor, *Bad*, selling over 32 million copies around the world.

The record was the first to be released under Michael's renewed recording contract with Sony (which had been brokered for $65 million – the highest amount that had ever been paid to an artist up until that point). Its first single, 'Black or White', stayed at the top of the charts for seven weeks and became an anthem for racial equality.

DANGEROUS

Release date:	26 November 1991
Producer:	Michael Jackson/Teddy Riley/Bill Bottrell
Singles:	'Black or White'; 'Remember the Time'; 'In the Closet'; 'Who Is It'; 'Jam'; 'Heal the World'; 'Give In to Me'; 'Will You Be There'; 'Gone Too Soon'

PLAYLIST:

'Jam'

'Why You Wanna Trip on Me'

'In the Closet'

'She Drives Me Wild'

'Remember the Time'

'Can't Let Her Get Away'

'Heal the World'

'Black or White'

'Who Is It'

'Give In to Me'

'Keep the Faith'

'Gone Too Soon'

'Dangerous'

KINDNESS AND CLENCHED FISTS

As with *Bad*, Michael's dual focus on chart success and charitable endeavour was a hallmark of the *Dangerous* tour. He established an organization named the 'Heal the World Foundation' (after the album's hit song) that donated millions of dollars to unfortunate children around the world on top of the remarkable feat of airlifting 46 tonnes of supplies to Sarajevo, the city that had been torn apart in the Bosnian War. Amazingly, Jackson donated all profits from the 67 concerts he performed at during his *Dangerous World Tour* to the foundation.

In another act which showed a combination of bravery and charity, Michael used the opportunity of his performance at Bill Clinton's presidential gala to highlight the issue of Aids and HIV, publicly asking for a commitment to research into the illness. As this was still a controversial issue at the time it showed a depth of integrity on Michael's part that he was prepared to publicly champion an issue in this way.

Alongside these acts of charity Michael performed an act that would go down in history as one of the greatest performances of all time: the half-time show at Super Bowl XXVII on 31 January 1993. Watched by nearly 135 million Americans, Michael's stage-show saw him seemingly disappear from atop a giant screen and reappear seconds later on a central podium, amidst an incredible display of fireworks. The moment was magical and the packed stadium exploded with excitement. For upwards of a minute, Michael stood perfectly still, fists clenched and eyes covered with sunglasses. Then, with anticipation at fever pitch, Michael removed his glasses and launched into a rendition of four songs, to the amazement and joy of everyone watching.

Under a month later Jackson was honoured with a Living Legend Award at the 35th Grammy Awards ceremony. With performances like this, as well as his stunning record sales and his generosity in the charitable arena, no-one could question the artist's eligibility for this stand-out recognition.

Opposite page and below left: **Michael visiting a Romanian orphanage as part of the 'Heal the World Foundation' in 1992.**
Below right: **On another charity mission, meeting traditional dancers from Entebbe School, South Africa.**

Michael's performance during half-time of Super Bowl XXVII forever changed the way in which the game was shown and set new records for viewing figures. For the first time ever, more people tuned in for the half-time performance than for the action of the game itself.

Right and following pages: **Michael's stunning performance at Super Bowl XXVII.**

Michael was in demand, from charity events to the Super Bowl.

3 Fall from Grace – the Wilderness years

As the 1980s rolled into the 1990s, Michael's incredible chart success was blotted by a string of rumours concerning his personal life. As someone fiercely devoted to his privacy, it was almost inevitable that Michael, like many other celebrities constantly under the spotlight, would be the subject of fascination and mystery, but aspects of his personal life – his purchase of the Neverland Ranch, his pet chimpanzee Bubbles, his often changing facial appearance and its gradual lightening in tone – would fuel curiosity. But more damaging than anything else was the accusation, raised in 1993, that Michael had behaved inappropriately with one of the young boys who visited the Neverland Ranch.

'I believe I'm one of
the loneliest people
in the world.'
– Michael Jackson

POP ROYALTY

Although the subsequent investigation and trial came to an end when it was settled out of court, the damage to both Jackson's career and health seemed irreparable. A portion of the *Dangerous* World Tour was cancelled and the combination of painkillers that Jackson had been taking to cope with the stress of the trial ultimately led to him spending a period of time in drug rehabilitation. For someone who had been so publicly and vehemently opposed to drug use throughout his career, this caused serious damage to the integrity of his public image.

Michael's marriage to Lisa-Marie Presley, daughter of Elvis, in May 1994 emerged as a result of her support for him during the trial. Although some sought to portray the marriage as an attempt to buoy up Michael's public image, the couple were committed to each other and remained close friends after their divorce almost two years later.

MAKING *HISTORY*

In an act that swept away the doubters and critics, in 1995 Michael unleashed his next world record-breaking project on his devoted fans: the double album, *HIStory: Past, Present and Future, Book I*. Featuring a selection of 15 of his greatest hits alongside 15 new songs, the release made a statement that Jackson was not only King of the past, but King of the future of pop. The album went straight in at number 1 and has since become the bestselling multi-disc album of all time, with over 20 million copies sold.

The album's second single release, 'You Are Not Alone', also won a record for being the first single to go straight to the top of the

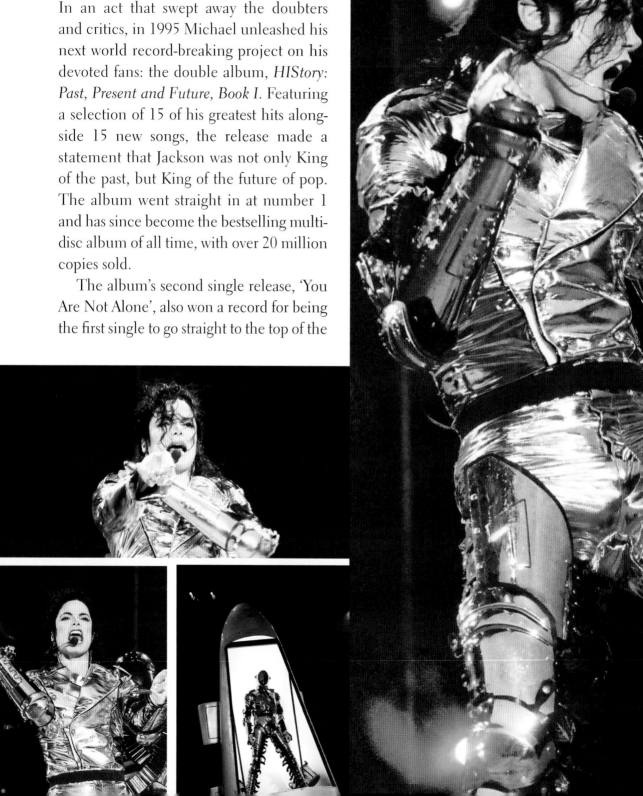

Billboard 'Hot 100' chart, while 'Earth Song', Michael's incredible plea for compassion for the world's poor and the environment, struck a chord with listeners worldwide: in the UK it sat at the top of the charts for six weeks, becoming his most successful UK single ever.

The tour for *HIStory* also set records of its own: travelling every corner of the globe, Michael performed in 58 different cities to a stunning 4.5 million people. While on the year-long tour, Michael released another record-breaking album – this time a set of remixes from *HIStory* entitled *Blood on the Dance Floor: HIStory in the Mix*. The album set a record as the biggest-selling remix album ever made, with sales of six million copies worldwide.

Backstage on
the *HIS*tory tour.

BECOMING A FATHER

It was during the *HIStory* world tour that Michael married second wife Deborah Rowe. The couple went on to have two children together: Prince Michael Joseph Jackson Jr. and Paris Michael Katherine Jackson. The couple divorced two years later in 1999, with Michael retaining custody of the kids, but remained on good terms.

Perhaps as a way to recover from the emotional ups and downs of the preceding years, Michael threw himself into his charity work, organizing and performing a string of benefit gigs with other top-name stars, the proceeds of which were channelled to the Red Cross, UNESCO and the Nelson Mandela Children's Fund. It's perhaps no wonder that a year later he was recognized by the *Guinness World Records* for his charitable work. He was awarded the record for the 'most charities supported by a pop star' with an incredible 39 organizations receiving his support.

Below left: **Michael with his second wife, Deborah Rowe.**

Below right: **Michael with another legend, hero and icon, the great Nelson Mandela.**

Performing 'Earth Song' at the
1996 Brit Awards.
On stage with Marcel Marceau
at the 12th annual MTV Video Awards,
Radio City Music Hall, New York.

INVINCIBLE

Ten years after *Dangerous*, Michael released his tenth and final studio album, *Invincible*. Despite the massive buzz of excitement surrounding the release of new material, its launch was shrouded amidst the controversy of the ending of his contract with Sony. Michael felt that as a result of his leaving the label, Sony had not pushed the album's release as much as they could have done; however, major promotional events did take place, including a celebration to mark Michael's 30 years as a solo artist. Taking place at the famous Madison Square Garden, a whole host of contemporary stars joined Jackson on stage, including the likes of Whitney Houston, Slash, Usher, 'N Sync and Britney Spears.

INVINCIBLE

Release date:	30 October 2001
Producer:	Michael Jackson/Rodney Jerkins/Teddy Riley/Kenneth 'Babyface' Edmonds/R. Kelly/Dr. Freeze
Singles:	'You Rock My World'; 'Butterflies'; 'Cry'

PLAYLIST:

'Unbreakable'

'Heartbreaker'

'Invincible'

'Break of Dawn'

'Heaven Can Wait'

'You Rock my World'

'Butterflies'

'Speechless'

'2000 Watts'

'You Are My Life'

'Privacy'

'Don't Walk Away'

'Cry'

'The Lost Children'

'Whatever Happens'

'Threatened'

'Success definitely brings on loneliness. It's true. People think you're lucky, that you have everything. They think you can go anywhere and do anything, but that's not the point. One hungers for the basic stuff.'

– Michael Jackson

Above left and centre: Michael performing at the 'United We Stand' concert, 2001.

Above: Michael at the 35th Grammy Awards ceremony with his sister Janet.

Michael performed at another concert very shortly after, but under very different, infinitely sadder, circumstances. Following the tragic events of 11 September 2001, Michael helped put together a charity event to commemorate those who died in the attacks, performing one of his own songs, 'What More Can I Give', alongside 35 other major artists who also gave their support and involvement to the subsequently released charity single.

Although *Invincible* sold fewer copies than his previous albums – a still astonishing ten million copies – it rocketed to the top of the US charts on its release and also hit the top spot in a dozen other countries around the world. It suffered a lukewarm reception with the critics, with many commenting on its length (around 80 minutes, with 16 songs), but with the bar having been set so high by his previous releases it was perhaps inevitable that anything less than a new *Thriller* would leave some fans and critics complaining.

RETIRING FROM THE PUBLIC EYE

After *Invincible* Michael began a gradual retreat from the public eye, spending more time at his Neverland Ranch. Although in 2002 he celebrated the birth of his third child, Prince Michael Jackson II, he shied away from revealing the identity of the baby's mother, and sought to keep the child, like his other two children, protected from the media gaze.

Despite retreating from public view, a 2003 TV documentary allowed cameras and reporter Martin Bashir into the Neverland Ranch to interview Michael in his home, gaining an unprecedented insight into his life. Just as a decade earlier he had been dragged into controversy, the documentary caused a storm of media interest for its supposedly incriminating revelations about the star's life. The allegations raised were denied by Jackson, who was publicly supported by many of his friends including actress Elizabeth Taylor.

A wheel had, however, been set in motion, and two years after the documentary aired Michael Jackson found himself in court in Santa Maria, California. An intensive trial period came to an end after five months with Jackson fully acquitted on all charges. Nevertheless, as before, the pressure on the singer took an immense toll.

Michael never failed to share smiles and autographs with his doting fans, even through the most difficult times in his life.

> '**Lies run sprints, but the truth runs marathons. The truth will win this marathon in court.**'
> – Michael Jackson

Above and below: Jackson's trial rapidly became a media circus but the support he received from friends like Rev. Al Sharpton, family such as his mother Katherine as well as his fans was immense.

Michael suffered from stress-related health problems and again found release through painkilling drugs. Perhaps as a direct consequence of the stress, Michael's appearance seemed further removed from the happy, dark-skinned child he had once been; fans who camped outside the trial courts to support Michael were greeted by an emaciated, pale shadow of his former self.

Following his acquittal, Michael escaped the glare of the media and spent time in Bahrain. In 2006, reports of financial insecurity became rife when it emerged that the main house on the Neverland Ranch had been closed down and that Michael had been delaying payments on a multi-million dollar loan.

The once mighty King, loved by millions worldwide, began to seem like a fragile, vulnerable child.

THE RETURN OF THE KING

Despite the turmoil of the years that followed the release of *Invincible*, Michael's ultimate return to form was something that no-one could deny. In 2006 he was awarded eight records by *Guinness World Records*, demonstrating his unique position at the top of the pop world.

Alongside these achievements, Michael was able to celebrate the landmark 25th anniversary of the first release of *Thriller*, doing so through the release of a new reissue album, *Thriller 25*. Another cause for celebration came in 2008 when Michael turned fifty. Sony BMG put out a compilation album entitled King of Pop to mark the event.

However, by far and away the biggest news of the last few years was the announcement that Michael would be returning to the stage and performing a series of concerts at London's famous O2 Arena.

KING OF POP
MICHAEL

THE CONCERTS
THAT NEVER WERE

In March 2009 Michael announced that he would be performing
50 concerts at the O2 Arena, scheduled for July that year.
The words he spoke to the screaming fans have a tragic echo:

'I'll be performing the songs my
fans want to hear. This is it, I mean
this is the final curtain call, OK?'

'My goal in life is to give to the world what I was lucky to receive: the ecstasy of divine union through my music and my dance.'

— Michael Jackson

SOME OF MICHAEL'S

• With the number I and number 2 ranked albums in the world (*Thriller* and *Bad* respectively) Michael was named the Entertainer of the Decade for the 1980s

• Michael won eight Grammy Awards in 1984 – more than any other artist has won in a single year

• Michael's contract with Sony Music for $65million, with possible earnings of $1 billion, was the largest ever brokered

• Michael's half-time performance at Super Bowl XXVII drew audience figures of 133.4 million

• Michael was paid a record $12 million for his involvement in four TV commercials for Pepsi Cola

• Michael's record-breaking world tour to promote *Bad* brought in over $124 million

• Michael was the first person in the charts' 37-year history to enter at the number I spot on the *Billboard* Charts 'Hot 100', with his single 'You Are Not Alone'

INCREDIBLE ACHIEVEMENTS

Bestselling video

• 'The Making of Thriller' is the bestselling video to have been released by an artist

Most *Billboard* 'Hot 100' Singles Chart number 1s

• Michael achieved 13 number 1 hits – the record for a male artist

Number 1 album debuts

• *Bad*, *Dangerous* and *HIStory* all debuted at number 1

Consecutive number 1 singles

• The Jackson 5 were the first ever group to have four consecutive number 1 singles

Number 1 on charts

• Michael claimed a new record in 1983 when he achieved a number 1 spot on the *Billboard* rock albums and rock singles charts, as well as the R&B albums and singles charts

Youngest vocalist to top the US singles chart

• Michael was just 11 when 'I Want You Back' was released

Most weeks at the top of the US album charts (non-soundtrack)

• Michael spent an astonishing 37 weeks at the top with *Thriller*

First entertainer to earn more than $100 million in one year

And ...

'Most successful entertainer of all time'
Guinness World Records

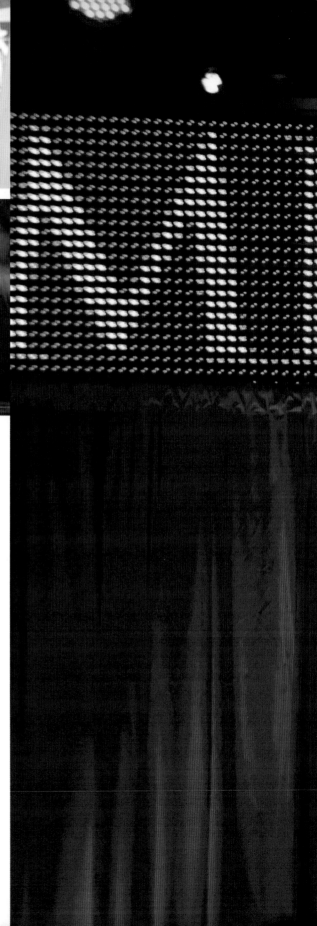

From top (clockwise): Fans queue patiently in line for a glimpse of their hero; Michael announcing the July concerts; in rehearsal - insider reports suggested the London performances would have been among Michael's finest.

Tickets for the first ten dates sold out within hours at a rate of around 11 per second, reportedly making it the fastest-selling show in history. Many saw the tour and arena concerts as a sure signal that Jackson was due a return to form and success – a reclaiming of his crown as King of Pop. For the hundreds of thousands of fans the concerts were to offer a dream come true – a chance to see their hero on possibly his last ever tour of the UK.

However, just days before the concerts were due to start, the world was shocked by a newsflash that no-one could have anticipated. Michael Jackson had died.

4 The news spread like wildfire.

Within hours internet sites, daily papers and radio and TV channels were reporting the same unbelievable news: Michael Jackson had died of a heart attack.

THE DEATH OF A KING

Michael had apparently collapsed at his home in Holmby Hills, California, and attempts to resuscitate him had failed. A paramedic crew arrived after receiving a 911 emergency call, but their frantic attempts to save him were unsuccessful. He was taken to hospital, but further attempts to revive the hero of millions met with no response.

What had happened? The world was in a state of shock and people everywhere were desperate for information. The media machine that had hounded Jackson for so much of his life went into overdrive, yet as swiftly as answers were unveiled came more mystery and confusion. In the following days the coroner's report showed that Michael had been shockingly underweight, seemingly exhausted and worn down by the strain of the upcoming concerts, but speculation as to what had prompted the cardiac arrest fed newspaper headlines for weeks.

Amid the scramble for information it seemed that a simple and honest truth had been lost sight of: the fact that a man, a father to three children, had tragically died.

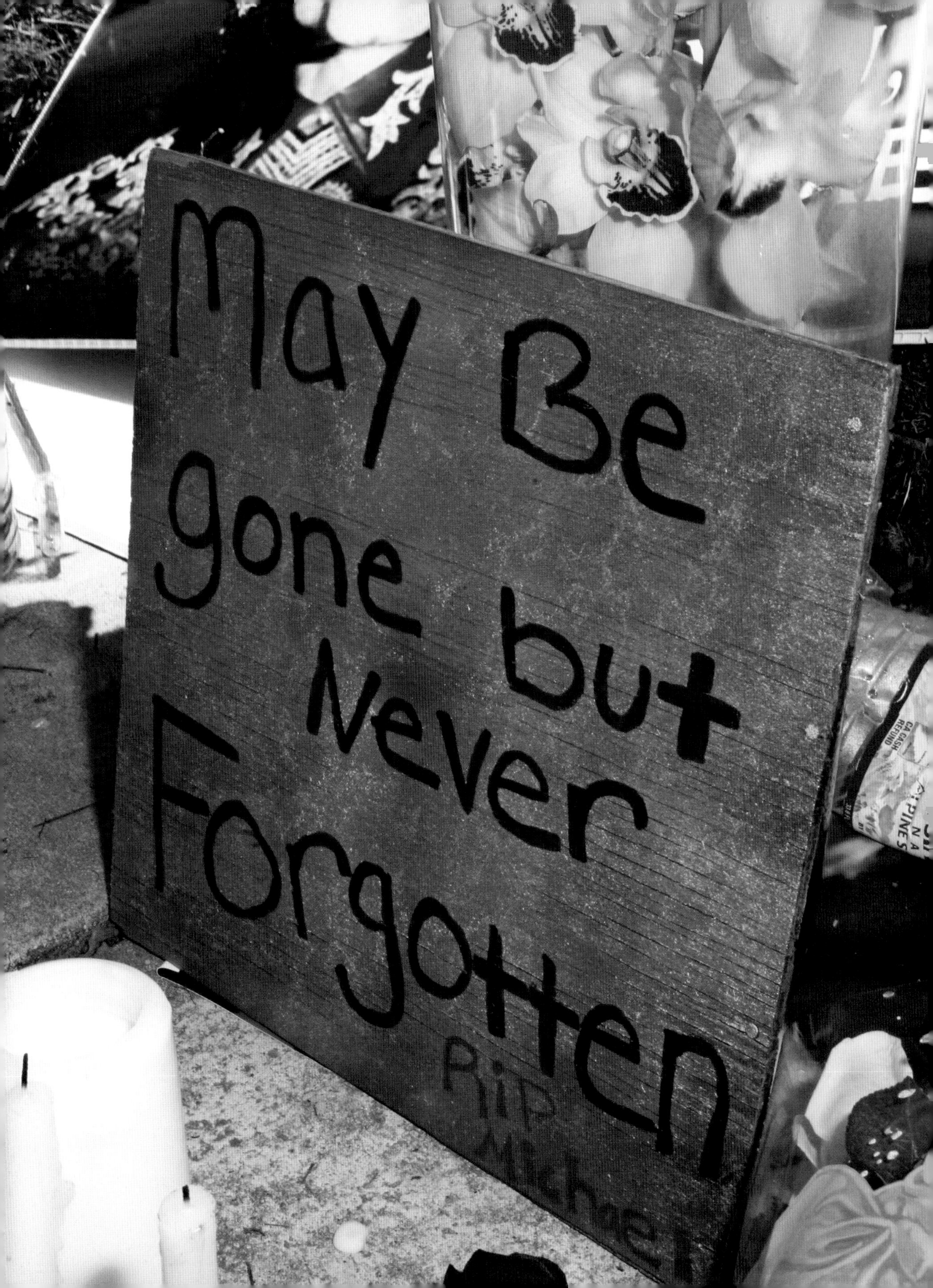
May Be gone but Never Forgotten
RiP Michael

After a lifetime spent in the spotlight, from childhood to middle age, Michael Jackson's death was no different. It was inevitable that the world's media would be hooked on every new angle to emerge from the tragedy. But while the fickle tides of popular opinion may change and the headlines follow suit, history will record a different story, and one that will last through time: that of a man who emerged from a humble background, who followed his dreams, nurtured his God-given talent and worked tirelessly to achieve his ambitions; a man who set records and helped millions with his acts of charity; a man who inspired and will continue to inspire hundreds of thousands of musicians across the globe; a figure who strode like a colossus across the world of entertainment.

A 30ft statue of Michael Jackson floats down the river Thames to promote the release of *HIStory*.

R.I.P.

MICHAEL JACKSON

the King of Pop

In the dark days that followed Michael Jackson's death, millions poured their grief onto internet chatrooms and forums, while many famous dignitaries and friends of the star were quick to give testimony to the effect he had had upon them.

REMEMBERING MICHAEL

'I am absolutely devastated at this tragic and unexpected news. For Michael to be taken away from us so suddenly at such a young age, I just don't have the words. Divinity brought our souls together on *The Wiz* and allowed us to do what we were able to throughout the '80s. To this day, the music we created together on *Off the Wall, Thriller* and *Bad* is played in every corner of the world and the reason for that is because he had it all … talent, grace, professionalism and dedication. He was the consummate entertainer and his contributions and legacy will be felt upon the world forever. I've lost my little brother today, and part of my soul has gone with him.'

— Quincy Jones

'He broke barriers, he changed radio formats.
With music, he made it possible for people
like Oprah Winfrey and Barack Obama
to impact the mainstream world.
His legacy is unparalleled.'

— Usher

'This was the most exciting collaboration
of my life with a man who has inspired
me like no other … This was the
world's greatest performer and the
world will miss him.'

— Kenny Ortega,
responsible for directing Michael's
cancelled London concerts

'I'm distraught.
I can't believe this could happen.
He was such a great character – a legend.
The news was such a shock.'

– Mohamed Al Fayed

'He inspired me. He taught me.
He laughed with me.'

– Whitney Houston

'From the beginning of my career
he was my idol in show business . . .
I had his poster on my wall.'

– Celine Dion

'It's so sad and shocking. I feel privileged to have
hung out and worked with Michael. He was a
massively talented boy/man with a gentle soul.
His music will be remembered forever and my
memories of our time together will be happy ones.'

– Sir Paul McCartney

'He was a role model, he was someone to cry to when my childhood was unbearable, he was a brother, he was a dear friend.'

– Corey Feldman

'I can't stop crying over the sad news. I have always admired Michael Jackson. The world has lost one of the greats, but his music will live on forever! My heart goes out to his three children and other members of his family. God bless.'

– Madonna

'We've lost a great entertainer and a pop icon. My thoughts and prayers go out to Michael Jackson's family, friends and fans.'

– Arnold Schwarzenegger

'My heart is overcome with sadness for the devastating loss of my true friend, Michael. He was an extraordinary friend, artist and contributor to the world.'

– Brooke Shields

'I'm still trying to hold on to the glimmer that it is not true. It is too surreal for me to absorb that Michael is no longer with us.'

— Uri Geller

'He was a kind, genuine and wonderful man. He was also one of the greatest entertainers that ever lived. I loved him very much and I will miss him every remaining day of my life.'

— Liza Minnelli

'I can't stop crying. This is too sudden and shocking. I am unable to imagine this. My heart is hurting. I am in prayer for his kids and the family.'

– Diana Ross

'Michael Jackson was my musical God.
He made me believe that all things are possible, and
through real and positive music. He can live forever!'

— Wyclef Jean

'Peace to the King … He was one of my childhood idols.
I salute you, King of Pop. You made the
whole world moonwalk together.'

— LL Cool J

'I was lucky enough to know and work with
Michael Jackson in his prime. Michael was an
extraordinary talent and a truly great international star.
He had a troubled and complicated life and,
despite his gifts, remains a tragic figure.'

— John Landis (the director of 'Thriller', the music video)

'I am very sad. No-one will be able to replace him. But I know that the light that he emanated from the stage will live on with all of us who saw him for what he was and always will be – a great teacher, pure musical inspiration.'

– Ricky Martin

'Michael Jackson showed me that you can actually see the beat. He made the music come to life! He made me believe in magic.'

– Sean 'Diddy' Combs

'To me, nothing is more important than making people happy.'
– Michael Jackson

This edition produced for The Book People Ltd,
Hall Wood Avenue, Haydock, St Helens, WA11 9UL

HarperCollins*Publishers*
77–85 Fulham Palace Road,
Hammersmith, London W6 8JB

www.harpercollins.co.uk

First published by HarperCollins*Publishers* 2009

10 9 8 7 6 5 4 3 2

© James Aldis 2009

James Aldis asserts the moral right to be
identified as the author of this work

A catalogue record of this book is
available from the British Library

ISBN 978-0-00-785902-3

Printed and bound in Great Britain by
Butler Tanner and Dennis, Frome, Somerset

PICTURE CREDITS

While every effort has been made to trace the
owners of copyright material reproduced herein,
the publishers would like to apologise for any
omissions and will be pleased to incorporate
missing acknowledgements in any future editions.

Getty Images: 13, 15, 18-19, 30-31, 33 (top left), 34,
36 (top right), 37 (top), 38 (right), 44 (right) 43 (right),
44, 45, 46, 47 (top), 50 (bottom right), 56, 58 (bottom),
59 (right), 62, 63 (bottom), 64 (top), 70-71, 72, 73, 74,
77 (top), 79, 82 (top right), 87 (bottom), 89, 95 (bottom),
101-2, 106, 108 (bottom left), 110, 111, 120, 124 (bottom
right), 126-7, 128-9, 133 (right), 136, 140, 141, 145
(top left), 151, 154 (bottom), 174 (bottom), 176, 181,
182-3, 185, 186, 190-2

Rex Features: 9, 20, 21, 22 (top), 23 (bottom) 35, 36
(top left), 37 (bottom), 38 (left), 43 (left), 44 (left),
47 (bottom), 48 (left), 50 (top), 51, 54, 58 (top), 62
(bottom middle) 66, 68, 69, 80-81, 83, 84, 85, 86, 87
(top left & bottom middle), 88, 92,93, 95 (top), 98
(left), 99 (bottom),100 (top right), 101 (far right), 104
(top),108, 114 (top & bottom left), 116-117, 118 (left),
122, 123 (bottom left),124 (top), 131, 133 (left), 137,
138, 142, 143, 144, 145, 153, 154 (top), 155, 157, 158,
159, 160, 162 (top & middle), 165, 170, 173, 174 (top),
177, 180

Press Association Images: 40, 82 (top left), 87 (top right),
99 (top) 104 (bottom right), 121, 161

Idols: 101, 123 (bottom right)

Corbis: 2, 10, 13, 14, 16, 17, 25, 27, 28, 29 (left), 33
(top right), 36 (bottom), 39, 52, 59 (left), 60-61,
63 (top), 65 (bottom), 77 (bottom), 82 (top middle),
90, 111-112, 146, 147-8, 166, 175, 178-9, 188-189

MJ.com: 29 (right)

Mirrorpix: 4, 22 (bottom), 23 (top and right), 48 (right),
50 (bottom left), 53, 98 (right), 104 (bottom), 108
(bottom right) 114, 118 (right), 119, 124 (bottom left),
125, 132, 134, 135, 150, 164

Celebrity Pictures: 169.